OUTHOUSE TO
WHITEHOUSE

Jimmy Mosley

Library of Congress Control Number: 2017956497
ISBN-13:   Paperback: 978-1-64151-174-2
             PDF: 978-1-64151-175-9
             ePub: 978-1-64151-176-6
             Kindle: 978-1-64151-177-3

Printed in the United States of America

LitFire
PUBLISHING

LitFire LLC
1-800-511-9787
www.litfirepublishing.com
order@litfirepublishing.com

CONTENTS

OUTHOUSE TO WHITEHOUSE

BIOGRAPHY

In this autobiography, the author paints a picture of what life was like to him, being a young black man growing up on a plantation in southern Mississippi. His journey in life would expose him to the racist practices within the infamous ceremonial unit-serving at the White House, as well as abuse witnessed firsthand on the plantations. Even in extremely difficult circumstances, this author overcame the odds. Jimmy Mosley (Author) shares how his faith in God, the wisdom taught to him by his single parent mother, and pure determination came to his aid.

His forty plus years of marriage, forty plus years of Military (uniformed) service to this country, and his commitment to God and family could serve as an example to be emulated in a time as this. I truly believe that each reader of Outhouse to Whitehouse will experience the presence of a Holy God. It wasn't a chance that my life would take me on a journey from having to experience the necessity of the plantations outhouse, and later serving at the nation's capital.

This book gives its reader a brief view of life on the plantations of the Deep South; without the many luxuries enjoyed by today's generation. The author's journey starts in a "shotgun" house on the plantation, and move on to the Whitehouse, and then tracks his life as the master educator. Outhouse to Whitehouse introduces its reader to extreme poverty, racism, the forgotten people living on plantations, and true commitment. The book is loaded with inspirational and informative events that are fit for Hollywood and could breed hope into America.

It is truly a message of hope and inspiration for its reader, and it forces you to realize just how blessed you really are. You won't be able to put her down once you have opened her pages. This could have been you.

ACKNOWLEDGMENTS

This book is dedicated to my mother, Mrs. Ophelia Brown, who I consider to be the world's strongest and wisest woman and truly God's gift to me. Written words are simply inadequate to express my gratitude for your love, prayers, and encouragement throughout the years. What I have learned from you has had the most profound impact on my life, and without your inspiration and motivation, this book might not have been published. This book will leave you thinking, *Could this really happen in America?*

The question *What could lead me to believe that this book,* Outhouse to White House, *needed to be published?* remains. It was the great need and desire for noteworthy experiences of past generations. Every reader will relate to some of the experiences shared in this heartwarming layout of the roads taken in this amazing masterpiece.

In addition to my mother, this book is also possible because of a second motivation, which came one day while relaxing under a shaded tree, from a good and trusted friend by the name of Raymond Dotson.

We were conducting routine training with our ROTC cadets outside the military drill pad, and the cadets were well into their drill daily sequence. Three of the cadets had gathered around Raymond and I as we were talking about how good kids have it today, in comparison to life when we were growing up. One thing that we both agreed on was the fact that kids today are totally unaware of the many benefits they have that are simply taken for granted.

We soon noticed that several young cadets were now seated around us, just seriously interested and absorbing our discussion of the old days. Raymond and I realized that we had the kids' undivided attention, so we kept the stories coming. Raymond and I ended up writing many tardy referrals that day as we totally lost track of time as the kids absorbed every spoken word about the old days. These cadets, along with other students, returned to our classroom during our lunch break to continue discussions and hear more details about earlier stories. These kids would not stop visiting our classroom over the course of the next few weeks, but Raymond and I decided to lock our doors in an effort to keep them from coming.

Raymond later said to me, "We need to document some of these events." The bottom line is that kids have a need to know about the generations before them and what they had to endure.

1

FORCED TO FIGHT
FOR A DOLLAR

It was my fourth year at L. S. Rogers Lavatory School, and lunch for the entire week cost only one dollar. Yes, we could actually eat a full-course meal for only twenty cents per day. Many of the city kids did not think very highly of a dollar, but for me, a paper dollar was a lot of money and something I really didn't get to see very often.

Gasoline back in those days cost twenty-six cents to the gallon at the country store, and I can recall walking to the country store with my bent-up gas can. We would cut the plantation owners' yard for a dollar fifty back then. You received change from a dollar after purchasing three hamburgers. This is the time line in the early sixties in the state of Mississippi.

If you did not have the twenty cents for lunch, the teachers would happily allow you to pull cafeteria duty. This meant emptying trays and you could eat free. Some kids brought their dollar to school in a tied-up handkerchief that had a knot at the end, and it was attached to their clothing. Inside the knot, the dollar was well secured. The day finally arrived when Mom could afford to give me a dollar.

Once cotton-picking season was over, Mom would begin to give us each a dollar. At this time, she had a second job cleaning houses for plantation owners. These were happy times. Happiness came to an end for me when J. D. Walker decided he wanted and needed my dollar more than I did. He would take my dollar on schedule every Monday morning.

I can recall JD's fist being about four inches wide, and he had been held back in the same grade three years in a row. He was the bully of all bullies and had the look of death in his eyes. I would not be the one to say no to JD. He had the build of an animal, and it seemed as if his fist dragged to the ground when he walked. He had placed the fear of death in my heart, so I would hand over my dollar to JD on schedule each week and ask for permission to work in the kitchen for my food; however, sometimes I didn't eat.

Somehow, Mom got word that I had not been eating lunch at school and that I had been giving JD my dollar. Mom was the only human being I feared more than J. D. Walker. She decided, after whipping me, that she would not continue to support JD's habit. I had prayed that JD would understand, but he continued to demand money and would put his hands in my pocket routinely, just to make sure my pockets remained empty of my dollar.

His routine consisted of his going into a rage, and he began to push me until he spotted a teacher nearby. I thanked God that the teacher was close by and alert. Nevertheless, JD decided to schedule a fight that day after school. The entire school heard about it and was excited and ready for the fight to begin when the bell sounded at the end of the day. It would be half an hour before the buses would arrive! This fight would take place under the large oak tree in the back of the school ground, and I had prepared myself to face death because there was no way I could come close to beating big JD in a fistfight. A few boys started pushing me in JD's direction as soon as the bell sounded. I had nowhere to run as I got closer and closer to that huge oak tree in which a group of boys gladly escorted me.

As they pushed me, I found myself inside this circle, with JD towering over me and pushing at will. As his meaty fist approached my face, I closed my eyes and waved my arms and wished for the best. I waited for the pain that never arrived. I open my eyes briefly to assess the damage; but to my amazement, JD was lying on the ground, where I assumed he must have stumbled.

There was this huge root from the oak tree sticking out of the base and from the ground. This was my opportunity to dive on top of him and not allow him to regain his balance or composure. The crowd declared me the winner that day, but in my heart, I still feared JD. I don't remember JD. attacking me ever again after that event.

This fight did a great deal for me in terms of enhancing my self-image and confidence. There must have been an unwritten rule of ethics for fighters because once you had scheduled a fight, you had the responsibility of getting the word out so that the crowd would know where to gather. There were primarily two ways of initiating a fight—putting an object on your shoulder and daring someone to knock it off and the other way was to draw a line in the sand or dirt and dare the person to cross it.

Meanwhile, this fight gave me a major confidence boost, and it brought me through middle school alive and lifted me up in the eyes of many other kids. The major point that I want every reader to know and understand is that in life, there are many JDs and we will always be involved in some type of fight. For some people, it may be a fight just to get up and go to work each day. For my family and me, our biggest fight was with being born into poverty.

My next fistfight would not take place until middle school, but I did advance to high school alive. My life took a major turn for the good when I entered into my high school years. This is when opportunities started to come my way. Life was still very challenging on the plantation, but I managed to secure employment through a summer school work program.

I received work for which I was qualified because of our family income status, and I then was hired through the school summer hire work program. I now faced the challenge of getting into the city each summer morning. I did have a bike that I had put together as a mode of transportation, but it was not anything that could be called dependable. The rear tires of this bike were stuffed with blue jean rags. The front tires had come from a racked motorcycle. I started riding this bicycle each morning to work.

I would leave home prior to daybreak each morning for a ten- to twelve-mile round trip. Approximately two weeks later, I had enough money to purchase new tires for my bike, and this made the ride much easier. In the city of Itta Bena, Mississippi, where I worked, I primarily cleared ditches, painted fences and roads, and mowed grass. This was a dream come true for me because working actually gave me joy and the opportunity to help my mother and the rest of my family.

Meanwhile, I would pass my family on my bike on the return trip from working in the city. They would pause for a moment from the fieldwork and wave at me. I was not aware at that time that I would continue to work several different jobs in the city and not have to return to working full-time as a field hand. I was earning a whopping $1.10 per hour. At the end of the summer, my family and I had the ability to move into town. We packed everything we owned and placed it on the back of Mr. Gibson's yellow pickup truck. We had to make three separate trips that day, but finally we became city folk.

This life experience could have been you! Times have changed but, in many ways, remain the same. If you visit the Mississippi's deep south, there are still families living in these conditions. America has the tendency of looking in far-off places for evidence of poverty, but there are still families out there, just like mine; and I thank God for the little help we did receive on the plantation in Mississippi. My question to you is, *Does America really want to help her own kind?* We really needed you, America.

I can recall my mother needing to take a few weeks off from the field hand work to give birth to my two younger sisters. She would chop—or "hoe cotton," as it is called—up until the last moment prior to giving birth, and she didn't complain. My grandmother, who was the country midwife, would always show up just in time to deliver all the babies. A lot of the records, birthdays, and papers got crossed up, but she worked as a midwife until she was well into her eighties.

After completing high school, I joined the United States Army and was headed into a totally different world. I was now a soldier and proud to be called a private. The sound of the name *private* really meant something to me because up until then, I had only been called *boy*. The US Army Infantry would become my new family.

My high school did not have a great program such as the JROTC. Our school was too poor and too small. I do not know what influenced me into joining the army, but my other friends and I were interested in the services and we decided to take the entrance examination in which we all passed. We joined to serve our country on the same day. I would be the only one of the five to remain in the armed services and make it a career. Drug addiction was the main reason behind the other four young men who did not remain in the military. Drugs were hurting youth then and still are a major problem. Each of the four young men has a sad story to tell.

My military career would take me on a twenty-plus-year journey. It was the easiest job I ever had and the most gratifying. My second career would allow me to teach JROTC while still wearing the proud military uniform.

This was a gift from God. I can look back and reflect on the entire process from start to finish and back to the present. It is abundantly clear as to how God moved me through each rung of the ladder.

I received a $2,500 enlistment bonus after completing basic training and advanced individual training. This money was in addition to my basic monthly pay. I had no experience from programs such as JROTC, and I somehow managed to learn what I needed quickly. This pay enabled me to send money home to my mom to help her take care of the rest of the family. The extra benefit of being in the infantry was that I have always enjoyed being and working outdoors.

2

STORMS CAME AND
TIME STOOD STILL

During periods of inclement weather today, we can simply pull out the generators and wait with flashlights and candles nearby. However, weather conditions should never be taken lightly and should be monitored closely on your weather stations.

We experienced many storms, and even to this very day I reflect back. Mom would always have us sit still and remain totally silent until the storm had moved over. She said God was doing His work and, if we didn't want to be struck down by lightening, we should sit as still as possible.

All the children would rush to the kitchen when the clouds moved in. We would secure all the available pots and pans and then wait and see who would be first to find leaks that would come from the tin roof when the rain started to fall. After finding the many leaks, we would sit quietly on the long wooden bench with a heavy homemade quilt on our laps. When the thunder and lightning became really loud and terrifying, we all covered our heads and remained quiet.

I suppose that this will sound a bit extreme, but it actually worked for us. It taught us a much-needed lesson in respect to God. Mom was not the smartest woman in the world, but her wisdom far surpassed our level of understanding. This was a woman who could heal any injury or sickness that we encountered while living on that plantation in Mississippi. She held the knowledge of the exact time to plant and how to use different plants in healing our bodies. I now realize that many of those homemade remedies are not recommended in this day and age, but the question remains—*Why did these remedies work back in those times?* Many of the old-fashioned remedies were passed down from one generation to the next; I suppose they go back as far as slavery times.

The most amazing thing I found is that they did work, and after applying the remedies, Mom would kiss us and tell us that we would be better in the morning. We believed and trusted in her words. I can recall only one actual doctor's visit during these times; this was when I had thrush on my tongue.

The local country doctor instructed Mom to place a bit of alum to my tongue so the bumps would go away. I remember not being able to speak for a few days. Whatever the conditions were, Mom always had a homemade remedy on standby. Could this have been an extra measure of God's grace, or were we just really lucky kids with a strong immune system? You can ponder on that a little while, but for me, there is no doubt God extended His amazing grace on us!

When I joined the army and started basic training (boot camp) at Fort Polk, Louisiana, I began sharing my plantation experiences with a friend whom I had met. He seemed to be very interested and would wait for me outside the barracks and very eager to hear me talk about the slave-like conditions. He once asked if I was a slave. I discontinued sharing my experiences with him after he expressed an interest in murdering the plantation owners and their families.

I personally had no problems with my upbringing because to me those were the good old days and God had provided all our real needs. Nothing could have caused me to have the thought of returning home to hurt anyone.

God had truly blessed us, and we had not missed a meal. We didn't eat steak, but we had plenty of preserved salted pork. You could actually go outside and find food everywhere—berries, trees weighed down with fruit, chickens, eggs, and rabbits all over. Mom would store a little of everything for the winter months ahead, but hog-killing time is what we children looked forward to.

Some of the men tractor drivers would show up with a gun in hand and sharp knives. Sometimes, we children would cry during the actual killing of the hog, primarily because we had made pets out of them. After shooting the hog, the men would hang the hog upside down, allowing the blood to drain. Then they would remove and sort out the innards. Now came the part we enjoyed the most—the scrapping off the hog's hair.

After dunking the hog in a barrel of hot, scalding water, the hair would scrape off quite easily. We would miss a hair spot or two here and there, but Mom would always supervise us closely. Then Mom would place rubber tires around the huge, black cast-iron pot for cooking the hog cracklings. We would sometimes take pockets of these cracklings to school, while our pockets would have these greasy large stains.

Time actually did appear to have stood still and was of little or no concern while living and working on the plantation. We considered sunup to sundown to be a full day's work. None of the field hands carried a watch or timepiece, but we knew when it was approaching quitting time. Normally, the boss man would show up about fifteen minutes prior to quitting time, and this would be our signal to start finishing newly started tasks.

Wake-up call was standard on the plantation. Each morning, the trusted rooster would crow about the same time of our daily wake-up call. The next wake-up warning would not be so nice because Mom would charge into the room, if she didn't hear us moving around, and no one wanted that.

Mom would have the breakfast ready. We would expect the boss man's truck to arrive no later than six thirty in the morning. He would proceed to blow the truck's horn, and we would rush out of the house and pile into the truck to be transported to a fieldwork site. Normally, the ride to the work site would be very short because the fields weren't very far apart.

Once everyone was in their assigned position for work, Mom would then position herself so she could monitor our work and ensure that we weren't leaving any grasses or weeds uncut. Many miles would be covered as each person would walk while chopping until they reached the end of the row of cotton, only to turn around and repeat that process over and over until the field was completed.

When the rain would catch us in the fields, we would run to the nearest tree for cover and try to avoid the lightning as much as possible. We all worked very aggressively as if we were working for ourselves. I am not really sure where the motivation came from, but that did not change the fact that we would be paid the same three dollars per day.

Maybe it was the ice-cold water Mr. George would bring us, or perhaps it was the five-cent moon pies he would give us if we finished a field in record time. We were more than faithful to our boss man. Sometimes, we would be so close to completing a field that we would actually want to continue working beyond our quitting time. When a situation like that would happen, the boss would generally take us by the store for soda pops.

You may be asking yourself what could motivate a person to become so committed and dedicated to a cause. What if a person could create, bottle, and sale such a product that would put this mind-set in each employee? One could very easily become a wealthy person if they could. How many eight-year-olds do you know these days who earned the same amount of money as their parents? I actually did match my Mom's paycheck, dollar for dollar. You may have noticed that I haven't made mention of a father. This is because I never met the man nor have I received any form of support.

I really did enjoy chopping in the tall cotton fields in Mississippi. The young girls made coming to work a true pleasure. I remember the day I noticed Ernestine for the first time, and the next days wouldn't come fast enough. I would hope that Mom would position me close to her and her family so we could quickly get ahead of the adult crowd where we would conduct small talk.

I was sure that she liked me as much as I liked her, so we started to sit together on the school bus. She would also visit the nearby well with her water jug, just to get me to carry it back to her house with her. Neither of us showed shame of the fact that we didn't wear shoes much of the time. Needless to say, our relationship didn't last because I was no match for the city boys.

These guys had money, knitted pants, and nice shoes. My shoes were being held together with clothes hanger wire. We would heat the hanger wire until it became red hot, and then we would burn its way through the sole and body of the shoe. We would proceed to clip and twist the wire with pliers. Many kids were cut as a result of the wire attached to shoes. One time, my dog returned home with a really nice shoe in mint condition, but he never found a match.

Mom would cut our hair with scissors, leaving large gaps. She would put a mixing bowl on our heads as she would cut around it. The kids at school called it the "'round the world" look. Kids really did make fun of us a lot. Thank God that we had a large family and my sister Odester could fight really well.

The world has gone and got itself into a big hurry. How I long to slow down. Whatever happened to the days when children could fall asleep in the tall grass or under a tree? I enjoyed watching my sisters playing mud cake under the house during the days that we weren't working. They would be at perfect peace as they waited for the mud plates to dry.

Even though cotton crops are not as abundant, they were when we lived and worked on the plantation. It is still possible to spot a few field hands driving through this part of Mississippi. The wages are not three dollars per day; they should not have been that meager then.

I believe we might have been a forgotten workforce. America forgot us, and they do a poor job of taking care of its own. Other families were just as poor as other families living on that plantation.

Eventually, we received cheese, powdered milk, and a box of used clothes. We were so excited to receive used clothes! Mom would get a ride into town and wait in a long line for a box of state-issued food. This was a big help because none of us received support in the form of money or stamps. It was God who supplied for us.

Times have really changed, but I will always enjoy reflecting. There is a danger in forgetting the past. Parents should continue to share these examples of the past with family and loved ones and allow them to see the amazing grace.

Turn off the radio, television, automobiles, running water, electrical power, and thoughts of the job while you give Him thanks and praise. Grab a heavy quilt with a cup of steaming coffee and just spend some time reflecting.

3

FIVE MILES TO ZION ROCK CHURCH

As I watched the actions of kids today, just moving around aimlessly on Sunday mornings, I can't help but reflect on the drills Mom put us through. My Mom "drugged" us to church every Sunday, and we were never given the option of staying home. Today, as I drive my family to church on Sunday mornings, I sometime think about the drills Mom would put us through as we prepared for church service.

Our drives home after church allow me to witness many activities from the vehicle windows that are even more astounding and everything but godly—loud music being played from automobiles with their windows down, people drinking and standing on the street corners, just to name a few. I have to ask, *What happened, America, to "In God We Trust"?*

The Bible says, "Train a child in the way he should go; and when he is old, he will not depart from it" (Prov. 22:6). Today, church is simply an option! When church is on television, children of this generation might quickly change the channel and parents do not talk about the Lord in their homes, except for the frequent use of His name in vain. When kids get together, they are talking about many worldly things. My question to every parent is, *How is the Bible taught in your home?* Here is my story.

While living on the plantation in Mississippi, my mom had many rules, but her number one rule must have been the one that made church attendance a mandatory event. Awakening to the sound of the rooster's crow at around 6:00 a.m., it was now time to get moving around the house. Eight bodies had to be washed using the two wash pans. We still had to eat and dress for church. We would not dare attempt to wear our Sunday clothes during the school week. This would just be the beginning of an action-packed day.

Our little church, Zion Rock, rested off the banks of a small lake call Blue Lake in Berclair, Mississippi. We often walked to Berclair for well water for drinking and grocery shopping at the only nearby country store. For all other water usage, we had to prime the pump that was located in our backyard. Pump water always started coming out of the pump a little rusty and hard, but sometimes we would still drink it. It was also an unwritten rule to never spill the priming water, which we sat aside for starting the pump.

Well, we really did have to walk to church on Sunday; rain, shine, or snow, we had to go. I can't ever remember having the option of staying home or not attending Sunday school class. We didn't have a radio, television, or telephone. However, we did have the spirit of the Lord in our hearts, and getting to that little church was the only option.

Mom was an authority figure who controlled her family and house with an iron fist, but on Sundays, she was a bona fide drill sergeant. You might say that she "drugged" us to church. Eight o'clock meant formation for inspection, and off we would go on a dirt-road march to church. During inspection, Mom would issue out the nickels and pennies with clear instruction that that money was to be put in the collection plate that would be passed around during morning and evening worship services.

Our preacher was a really big man who enjoyed eating at the member's home after preaching. I slept through most of his performance-based preaching while all the time thinking about the two snow cones I would buy after church. I had learned from my brother how to seemingly tap the nickel to the bottom of the collection plate while retaining the coin in my hand. Anticipation made the walk back home seem really long, but the snow cones, which came in only two flavors, were really tasty.

Sundays were really a day of resting and feasting. The church mothers would take turns feeding the preacher each Sunday after service. When my mom would feed him, it was a really big event. Perhaps, there was a degree of competition among the mothers of the church. We had to clean the house, rake and clean the yard, and stand watch for the preacher and his entourage. Of course, the deacons and their wives would follow.

After all the adults had finished eating and talking, the children would then be allowed into the kitchen. We would attack the pies and cakes first. After eating, we would change out of our Sunday clothes for outside games. We played many games as a family but always after church services were completed.

I recall my sister would get really upset when we would remove the heads from her doll, but we needed a ball. We would play hopscotch, skip rope, jackstones, dodge ball, and sometimes hide-and-seek in the cotton and bean fields. There was never a boring moment. Other children from the plantation would come over, and we would play until dark. Sundays were truly a Sabbath day of rest, eat, and play in our household.

At the tender age of eight, I completed my two weeks on the mourners' bench and was baptized. During "mourning," members would come forward, gather around us, and put hands on us in prayer.

This would continue each night for two weeks. It was now time to take that walk down the freshly cut path leading down to the grassy waters. We would file down the path and wait in the shallow water until the deacons led us out to the preacher one by one. I was really glad when this was over.

Zion Rock still stands today. I always visit this church when I am home on vacation, and the Word is richly presented. Mom is still a committed member of Zion Rock Baptist Church in Berclair, Mississippi. If you were to go there now, you would not find the paper fans, outhouses, wasps, and other various insects found inside as much. The improved condition of the church provides much comfort.

I often reflect back on all the good times I have had in that little church. It is really something special about being trained up in God's house. Thank you, Zion Rock!

4

JUST IMAGINE—THE FIFTIES ON A MISSISSIPPI PLANTATION

Just for a moment, imagine living on a "boss man" plantation in the Deep South in the early fifties in the state of Mississippi. Inside your living quarters are no running water, no indoor plumbing, and neither gas nor electric appliances. We actually lived in what was called a shotgun house. A shotgun house is a house you stand in the front door and look through the back door at the same time. *Small* is a kind word to describe a shotgun house. These houses were used to house the field hands, which will also be referred to as "hoe hands."

When it rained, there would be numerous leaks where water would come into the house. In addition to the many leaks, the screened windows and doors had tears, and this made it difficult to keep the insects outside. Then came the nighttime.

Mom would light the coal oil burning lamp to provide light until everyone was safely in bed. It was especially important that each of us carefully moved around in the dark room because we really didn't want to knock over the "pee can." This was actually a white pot with a plastic lid cover and was used for minor bathroom pit stops. Other "pit stops" would require a visit to the outhouse, which was nothing more than a fixed bathroom contracted from wood boards and located out back, away from the house.

Inside our living quarters, you could find two large lumped beds positioned in each corner of the room—one cotton lumped bed for males and the other for the five females, each sleeping head to foot. Many would say that these were slave-like conditions, but we felt blessed.

Today, there are numerous luxuries that are simply taken for granted by our youth, and they need to know that something positive came from an event or life experience. A good example of a luxury that is often taken for granted would be toilet paper; we rarely had any when I was growing up. We had the large Sears and Roebucks' catalog as the paper of necessity, and we never complained.

The catalogs would arrive once each month, and Mom would find extra copies when she would clean the house for the plantation owners.

We often daydreamed as we looked at the items on the pages torn from the catalog, I can recall the warm feeling of almost experiencing what it would be like to actually have the items I daydreamed about. Those were years when being black and living in the backwoods of Mississippi could have been an eye-opening experience, but we still felt blessed.

Assistance from the government may have been available; but other than the peanut butter, powdered milk, and canned meat, I can't recall much help from government or church groups. Today, you can find many assistance programs. However, for my family, we did not know how to go about obtaining the assistance; but my mother did her best.

Mom had to do extra work on the plantation to make ends meet. I don't ever recall having any means of transportation, with the exception when we rode in the back of the boss man's pickup truck. He would sometimes take us to the country store where Mom always kept a running tab. The store was actually located about five miles from where we lived, but we would walk and sometimes run all the way, depending on the level of excitement.

Today, a kid will walk past a penny, but not us. I dreamed of having a large family for the primary purpose of having many hands to work on the plantation, and this equaled more money. If my remembrances are correct—and I believe it is—we were paid a sum of two dollars per day for each family member working on the plantation. The average age for a kid to start chopping (hoeing) and picking cotton was around eight years old. There was a part of my growing-up experience that I regret when I reminisce, and that's not standing up for the females who were physically and sexually abused at times.

During the rare times when we were not working, males were sent to the store for a strange reason, so the sons of the plantation owners would be left alone with the females. Females were taken advantage of, and the sad fact was, everyone looked the other way. It seemed as if the city kids had everything—the nice clothes and store-bought shoes—while we had only hand-me-downs. Our shoes were held together with coat hanger wire.

Outhouse to White House focuses on the true meaning of happiness, love for family, and the awesome heart of God. Each reader will take a peek into the past and view life through the eyes and heart of a true survivor of hard times—me! You will see my life's journey from the very start in that small town in Mississippi called Itta Bena. There you will be introduced to poverty, face to face.

Many of our basic needs were not being met, but it was the grace of God that kept us safe and healthy. The abandonment of the father and no positive male role model to look up to is another issue addressed. You may have a problem believing in some events, and some of the terminology might be outdated and only used on the old plantations.

Throughout all the struggles and sacrifices, this family endured. We still found laughter and enjoyment even without the luxury of television, radio, and telephone.

5

THE HUMAN COTTON PICKER

Work ethics aren't something with which a person is born; but I believe my mother planted a strong work ethic in me, without her ever realizing what was taking place. Mom would let others know in a heartbeat that she was proud of me and how hard I would work. While those spoken words actually motivated me, they caused me to excel.

I needed that special attention from Mother. Mom would put me in a cardboard box, which had been padded with a blanket, while she picked cotton. She told me that the pet dog was a wonderful guard dog, and it would not allow anything like snakes to approach my box.

It wasn't long until I would realize that picking cotton was my talent. No other eight-year-old on the plantation could measure up to my raw ability to swiftly grab the cotton from the bush and place it inside the sack until the sack was filled. I didn't ever think picking cotton was actual work for me because I enjoyed being the one getting all the glory and uplifting words from Mom. To some degree, this is where I obtained the label as the cotton picker.

Then came the problem with my not being able to awake at night to visit the urinal pot. Normally, my mom would whip any child who wet the bed; but in my case, she would make an exception because she felt that I worked until I became exhausted. My elder brother, Man, had the assigned duties of waking me up and ensuring that I didn't wet myself, but even his best efforts failed. He received many whippings for my error; I think he may have gotten a bit angry at me.

The picking cotton routine worked pretty much the same as chopping, in terms of transportation. The pickup truck would arrive about the same time each morning, and we would continue until sunset. Each morning, the field hands would pile into the pickup, as many as would fit. Sometimes the boss would have to make several trips to get all the families to the field site.

Everyone of age would grab a sack and move to their assigned row, and this would be the start of our first sack of cotton from that day. I had a set of specially made kneepads to protect my kneecaps, but because I could work so aggressively, I was able to strip a stalk of cotton every few seconds. What a boy! I could make as much as four dollars a day, at the rate of two cents per pound. This was a little better than chopping cotton in that it allowed a person to make more money.

Chopping cotton had its set price of two dollars per day where a person could make as high as four to six dollars each day picking. We would just about do anything to increase the weight of our cotton. I recall pouring water onto my cotton while some would even do the unthinkable—urinate on the cotton, just to get the extra pound of weight.

When school was in session, my family and I sharecropped, which simply meant we worked section of fields and received payment at the end of each year. After school, when our workday would actually be just starting, we had to work in the field or garden until dark and then we would complete any school homework assignments.

Mom kept a running tab of all the cotton bales we would pick, and at the end of the year, we would receive a cash settlement. While working in the fields each day, after returning home from school, we were able to clear fifteen bales one year. We watched Mom count the five hundred dollars over and over. We paid our debt at the country store and had extra money to spend. Mom never felt cheated, used, or abused, although she may have been.

Along with picking cotton, chopping, and pulling up weeds, there was plenty of work available. Contrary to families of today, my family did not have to deal with body weight problems; we were all slim, trim, and fit.

Mom did not pay much into social security during her work history because of the way laborers were paid back in those times. My mom has over sixty years of working, providing for her family. She has to now live on a substandard amount of social security and SSI that, combined, equaled to $495.00 per month; $200 went to mortgage payment. My mom will receive just payment for all her hard labor in heaven someday.

Even though we failed to comprehend what is actually taking place in our lives, nevertheless, the seed for success was being planted at a rather early stage. Whether it's Mom talking baby talk or entering you into a pie-eating contest, just take a brief pause and reflect for a moment. We will all have a yearning and passionate desire to gain others' approval.

I wished many times that I had not sent my mom the picture that I own of my prospective soul mate. This picture was the single most valuable item that would give me the most needed motivation to survive army boot camp. This was something tangible that I could focus on during the twelve- to fifteen-mile forced marches.

I actually wanted Mom's approval. This need ranks close to the top of man's priority list. I knew my mom would boast and show my picture to the other church members. It was as though I had found a pot of gold and soon I would be able to go on this huge shopping spree.

Mom molded me into that human cotton picker. To the young, I ask the question, *What will you become?* To the older generation, I ask the question, *Did you become what you desired to become, or did you get caught up in the cotton-picking mold?*

6

IN HER DARKEST HOUR, SHE CRIED

To hear such a stern woman as my mom crying in the late hour of the night was something I was not ready for. What could bring this woman of iron to tears?

While sitting at the kitchen table, somewhere between the hours of ten and midnight, I heard the sound of crying coming from my mom's bedroom door. I had dressed myself heavily to cushion the whipping she had promised me earlier that day for a reason of which I wasn't really sure. As I quietly sat and waited my punishment, her bedroom door opened, and she momentarily questioned my motives for being up.

I had known that it wasn't a good idea to go to bed thinking she would forget her promise to discipline me. Mom would snatch the covers off the bed and whip your backside but only when she felt good and ready. She never operated from a whipping schedule, but she kept her promises right. To my surprise, the whipping ended rather quickly. This was not normal procedure for my mom. She normally would talk to you and insist that you not attempt to protect your face during the actual course of the beatings.

I often felt that my mom had this huge bundle of pain that needed to be released as she would sometimes whip the entire clan, if no one would fess up and tell her the truth. I would often fight to get to the end of that line. I hoped that she would grow tired, but Mom had the arm of a baseball pitcher. She could complete the entire whipping line with only one break.

I personally had not been the type of person who would show emotions of love easily, but I suppose that that came as a result of the way I was raised as a child. I could show many acts of kindness, but to say the actual words *I love you*—this was a challenge, which I still wrestle with this very day. I recall crying, and it would take hours to calm myself. To fail at anything would be a sign of weakness, and that was not an option for me. The fear of failure would consume me as I would attack every challenging aspect of my life with such passion.

This can-do attitude would take me far in every major area of my life—my marriage, my job, as a father, and as a family man. I valued winning and had a need for success. It was Mom who planted that seed of passion and determination in me.

Every mother wants their children to have a better life than they had. To not be able to provide for that child's basic needs would be very painful. God was so very good to us. He met us where we were and gave us joy. The next time I saw my mom cry was at the funeral of my second eldest sister, Odester Smart.

Mom tried to read from the Bible, but tears flowed so strongly down her face, making it impossible for her to continue. She did get through the words "Let not your heart, be troubled." I helped her through the rest as I had memorized John 14:1–4:

Do not let your heart be troubled. Trust in God: trust also in me. In my father's house are many rooms: If it were not so, I would have told you. I am going there to prepare a place for you. And if I go there to prepare you, I will come back and take you to be with me that you also may be where I am. You know the way to the place where I am going. (NIV)

It was one of those moments God allowed me to be calm and at her side. Mom had referred to Odester as her baby. Mom retired from her job at Mississippi Valley State University to fulltime caregiver to Odester. Mom watched her take her last full breath in that hospital bed in Greenwood, Mississippi. I thank God for allowing me to be there for Mom.

I call Mom a "woman of iron." I can say Mom was a woman of iron because she had strength that could have only come from God Almighty. She raised five girls and two boys completely alone. There was no public assistance, child support, or help from a husband. There was no luck involved either. Mom had chickens by the hundreds, pigs, hogs, and a large garden to support her family.

We found something to do on the plantation, whether we were in or out of season. The entire family worked together, and no one stayed home. If you happened to be too small to chop or chuck or pick the cotton, then you would simply wait in the cardboard box at the end of the cotton rows until the crowd could make a round.

Sometimes the dog would provide security for the babies. We would all share in the details around the house including slopping the hogs, feeding the chickens, and collecting eggs. Sling blades were used to cut and hoe the grass. There were picking of blackberries and shelling both peas and beans. Canning was done to cover the winter months. I have been asked many times, "Were you a slave?" You be the judge.

After cutting stove wood and slopping the hogs and feeding the chickens, we were off to school. We did not have the luxury of preschool as children of today have. This placed us at a disadvantage in the educational arena.

Mom would make sure that we had plenty of brown paper bags to secure our lunch for each day. The grease stains at the bottom of the bag would let everyone know what was inside. Twenty cents were a bit much to pay for cafeteria lunch. Therefore, between sack lunches and emptying trays during lunch detail, we managed to never miss a meal. My family never went hungry for lack of food. There was food everywhere in the garden—numerous vegetables, different fruit trees, and mudbugs to eat. Mom would make and leave homemade biscuits in the wood-burning stove for us.

It was natural to go barefoot while working in the fields. The only exception would be when the dirt became too hot and unbearable. If you cut yourself from the hoe blade, this would require the wearing of shoes. I would never recommend this to anyone today.

I would realize that it was God's grace that brought us through the hard times in rural Mississippi. There was not even one snakebite from picking berries in the ditches, and we saw plenty of snakes. We sold our berries for fifty cents per gallon to the boss man's wife.

We would often kill a hog and salt down the meat to preserve it. It seemed as if food never spoiled in those days, and medical doctors were never in demand. I do not remember visiting any doctors who lived in the city.

Digging in the dirt was a fun hobby for all of us kids. We would find coins and run the three to four miles to the nearest store and purchase penny candy. All of us children played mud cake under the house. We would wait until the mud dried and became hardened. Sort of sounds like the perfect family. We had our share of fighting among ourselves and getting into trouble sometimes.

Mama would make us hug and say we were sorry to each other after the fighting. If we used profanity at the time, then that was a different story. She would put soap in our mouths as punishment.

I could go on and on about the hard and difficult life we spent on the plantation that shaped me into the person I am today. I have only one wife, one child, and, most important of all, one purpose—to serve God. In the forty-plus years on this earth, I have not been involved in any type of serious trouble including never having a traffic ticket. I thank God for His grace on me!

7

A SECOND CHANCE—
HE GAVE ME

I needed to fit in, and that need almost destroyed any chance of my having a career or future in the United States Military. Many of the decisions I make even today are filtered through a system developed as a result of a single mistake that could have altered the course of my life.

It was after boot camp, and this would be the beginning of my life as a real solider. My first assignment would be at a military base in Fort Hood, Texas. Upon my arrival to my assigned company, I quickly noticed that all of the soldiers were missing. They were on a field training mission in the local military training area, and I had the entire barracks to myself.

Many of the guys with whom I would be working had served in the Vietnam War, and I had no idea what to expect from these seasoned veteran soldiers. The sergeant on duty assigned me a bunk, a wall locker, and footlocker and told me that I was restricted to the barracks and could only go to the mess hall at mealtime. The barracks was located on the third floor, and I had the top bunk located toward the rear of this large open bay.

There was absolutely zero privacy in these open living conditions. The bathroom was located at the floor entry where the toilet bowls were about eighteen inches apart and in a single row of six. The shower had a large drain in the center of the floor with water sprockets mounted on the walls. At this point, I only wanted to keep my nose clean and be the best soldier I could be.

Everything appeared to be on track until the veteran soldiers returned from their field training. These guys had green paint all over their faces and several layers of dirt caked on their uniforms. They were very loud, playful, and aggressive with each other. Profanity was very commonly used by most. Some of the guys stayed in the motor pool area to wash down the APCs (armored personnel carrier) while the crew who came to the barracks would be responsible for cleaning the platoon's weapons. They soon completed the details, cleaned the vehicles and weapons, and started taking showers. After everything was accounted for; alcohol, drugs, and gambling would become the activities of the evening.

Dice were being rolled on the tight blanket of the bottom bunkbeds. The card games were now in full gear, and a cloud of smoke from the illegal substance filled the room. I could hardly breathe from all the smoke. Some guys would roll their own weed from their personal stash. You might be asking yourself, *Where are all the supervisors?* That was the way it was! To a new, young naïve recruit, it appeared as if these activities were all standard and legal, so I just continued to take everything in.

Around eight o'clock that evening, I walked over to a group of veterans playing cards on a footlocker across my bay area. As I stood and looked over their shoulders, one guy suddenly handed me his joint without even giving me a glance. Although I was amazed, I knew that this was a test. I had to make a decision at that moment.

If they felt that I was a spy, they may have possibly thrown me from the third-floor window. I reached out and accepted. I pretended to inhale the first few times. However, at some point, I must have actually inhaled as well as picked up the wrong beer can. I became the life of the party that evening.

The veterans surrounded me. They laughed and encouraged my telling jokes. I found out later that the sergeant had spiked his beer with acid and I picked up the wrong can and lost my inhibitions and fear.

I felt accepted into the group and would accompany a few guys to the enlisted men's nightclub. We took the party to the enlisted men's club located a few blocks from our barracks. In just a few short hours, I would be in a military jail.

The stage was in place for disaster at any moment. My long, black military coat swayed from side to side as I danced alone to the music. The song on the jukebox had me keyed up as I danced to the lyric of the song "Kung Fu Fighting."

As I danced, the alcohol started to make me feel a little sick. I found myself seated alone at the table. The other guy had scored a date for that night, and I was once again alone. However, I did have one full pitcher of MD—codename "Mad Dog Wine"—remaining on the table. Mad Dog became my loyal companion that night as I secured her for our walk back to the barracks.

Suddenly, blue lights surrounded the area, and I found military police (MP) all over me. The MPs grabbed me from behind, but I was able to slip right out of my long, black raincoat. Feeling very cheerful and energized, it was time to put in action my level of fitness which I trained so hard to obtain. I recall running and being chased by a few MPs. I also knew that the police had little to no chance of catching up with me. I continued my military maneuvers until I no longer could see anyone behind me.

I needed to return to the club to refill my pitcher of Mad Dog that had spilled as a result of the chase. This proved to be a mistake and major flaw in my impaired state of mind. Within minutes, the police spotted the mud spots on the back of my coat and knew that I was their guy. Five MPs restrained me, and I would spend time in jail until my commander or first sergeant could come and sign for my release. This turned out to be a long night because I still had a little fight remaining in me. After getting sick inside the cell, I soundly went asleep, lying in my own vomit.

Saturday morning arrived, and my first sergeant showed up to sign my release forms. I remained speechless as I attempted to assess the level of damage caused and the effects that it would have on my employment with the military. After I had showered and shaved under the supervision of my assigned squad leader, I was scheduled to go before the "old man" (commander) at 1600h for reading of the rights and (UCMJ) punishment.

I would spend the next six hours practicing how to report to my commanding officer and conduct punishment procedure. "Sir, Private Mosley reporting as ordered"—these six words were vital as I practiced putting my uniform headgear under my arms prior to knocking on his office door. I had to get that right because that would be my only chance to make a lasting first impression.

The reporting went well; I stood three steps from and centered to the company commander's desk. Procedure went as explained by my chain of command until the commander asked me the last question prior to administering punishment.

"Son, what were you drinking?"

I quickly responded with "Mad dog, sir!"

This response released me from all forms of UCMJ actions. The commander ordered me to return to my barracks and never come before his desk again. My military performance suddenly shifted to an all-time high.

I received best dressed private and best detail man awards. I would wake up fifteen minutes earlier just to be ready to serve. I have never tasted a drop of MD 20/20 since that incident. At some point in life, we all have been given a second chance to get it right.

My question to you is quite simple—*Did my commander make the right decision?* My action could have ended my services to this great country with an article 15 in my military records. (An article 15 allows for a commanding officer to decide the innocence or guilt and administer punishment to an offender where a minor offense does not require a judicial hearing.) I became a first sergeant later in my career, also offering second chances and clear instructions to several newbies to never appear before my desk again. I really thank you, commander, for that second chance.

8

PROVE THAT YOU REALLY CARE ABOUT ME

"They don't care how much you know, until they know how much you care," the saying goes. Children these days are not impressed by the number of degrees the teacher may have. The fact of the matter is that some children have never been taught respect for any form of authority, so teachers and leaders must turn to skills that allow them to win the student over. How can an educator be expected to reach a child who will not yield or show respect for authority?

For a newly assigned teacher fresh out of the military, how hard could dealing with kids be? Well, I found myself in an environment filled with students who had no prior experience in areas of humility, submission, or restraint. This is when I first learned that I couldn't win with force on force, especially when put in a position where there are no real powers with which to fight. I had my twenty years of military experience, but I needed to apply something different if I was to be successful in this position of being a teacher.

In the military, with each position came the necessary inherited power; but as a teacher, I couldn't drop the students for push-ups, suspend pay, or issue article 15's for acts of disobedience. At first, this situation had me as confused as a deer caught in the headlights of a car, until I met Ray. I'll call this particular student "Ray," but do understand this is a real event.

Ray did not come to school to learn, but he did come to obstruct all and any manner of learning that might take place in the classroom. Ray would argue with anyone who didn't look the way he thought they should, he would drum on the desk, pull females' hair, and start fights when possible. Many students had requested new seating arrangement just to get as far as they could from him, while others were simply afraid of him.

I knew that I had to find a solution to this growing problem, and I needed to act fast so that I didn't lose my entire power base. After pondering many hours on what actions to take, I finally presented the problem to my better half—my wife—and she said. "Give him something to do." The very next day, I called Ray to the side and asked him to help me control the class and to take on the responsibilities of class leader. But I forgot to mention anything to Ray about his use of profanity.

It was as the students were entering the class and I was monitoring from outside my door that I heard Ray applying his assigned authority—all the wrong way. Now I had to take Ray and teach him a lesson about respect being a two-way street, which implies that he must give it first. This would become Ray's job; he was now my inside student while I monitored movement in the class. Ray soon moved his small desk right up beside my desk. Ray's added responsibilities would be to monitor class starter activities and write names of students talking on the board for me while I completed attendance cards.

I knew that I had won Ray over when he stood up one day and shouted out, "Be quiet, the sergeant is talking." I now had a class leader, and the other students actually listened to him for reasons I wasn't really sure about. Ray never really participated in learning, but he asked me if he could get a grade for rapping instead of presenting a speech in front of the class. The class found his talent to be amazing as it appeared that Ray had been totally transformed into a respectable young man. Ray gave me that needed direction during my first years as an unarmed teacher.

The message to you is quite simple—"Kids don't care how much you know until they know how much you care." Ray became a model squad leader that school year, and he would actually catch himself when he felt profanity was about to come out. I later learned that Ray's mom was a single parent, just like my mom. His mom noticed a big change in his overall conduct, even though she had to stop him from using my name so much around the house.

Teachers and leaders can both learn a lesson from this experience because they usually are task oriented rather than people oriented. We shouldn't just use people to achieve a goal, but we should actually love and serve those whom we seek to win over.

9

THE DREAM TEAM CONNECTION

In September 1994, after completing a successful twenty-year career with the United States Military, I would now have the privilege of working with four of the most professional instructors whom I have ever encountered. These four individuals had also retired from the military and were now into their second careers as ROTC instructors at the high school level. We had a total of five instructors at C. E. Byrd—four first sergeants and one officer.

I accepted the position as an instructor/teacher after only a three-minute interview with the school principal. My first mission would be to prove myself worthy in this new field, and in doing so, it was my intention to make myself available and ready to pull my share of the workload. It took me a period of time to learn to speak the civilian language, but prior to grasping it, I made a few innocent mistakes.

I recall my first week getting used to the school's lunch schedule. This was a real challenge for me because in the military, we were given almost two hours, which allowed time to go home and eat. Well, I did go home, and when I returned, the students were in my room, unattended. The event wouldn't take place for another few months.

Jack Mitchell, who was part of my chain of command, had been monitoring my every move; and he decided to give me a day off. To my amazement, he informed me that I would have Friday off. I was really excited; and in my mind, I thought this meant I didn't have to come to work at all the next day, so my wife and I packed our bags and went on an extended weekend trip out of town. This was a huge mistake. I did not know his definition of the word *off*.

My fellow coworkers had attempted to reach me at home and students were gathered at my door, but I could not be reached. We all had a big laugh about the incident, and I did learn the true meaning of his use of the word *off*, which is to reduce an individual's workload. What an adjustment I had to make in living and working as an ex-military soldier. We finally did all get in step, and together we took our program to another level of excellence.

The C. E. Byrd Army JROTC program advanced forward and won the Distinguished Sweepstake trophy for ten consecutive years. This school would receive the blue-ribbon recognition from the White House. Our school records will reflect this time span from 1994 to 2004. No other school within the Caddo Parish, Louisiana, area would have their name engraved on this particular trophy. There would be only one name to be found—C. E. Byrd Army JROTC. This was the result of total commitment and dedication shown by the instructors and student cadets.

What am I alluding to with this story? Could it be possible that this came about by a divine intervention? This is the rest of the story.

During the annual JROTC Sweepstakes Award banquet, this trophy is awarded. The school's JROTC program is ranked in the following five areas: orienteering, physical fitness, male and female drill teams, rifle marksmanship, and the color guard. Each school within the Caddo Parish district competes. The judges tally all the scores within the abovementioned areas. The team with the largest total is declared the winner.

It is my opinion that God's favor was on the C. E. Byrd JROTC program for those ten consecutive years. The instructors took the initiative to start each school day with Bible study. This would include reading scripture, prayers, and a review of the day's training plan. Meetings were promptly started at 0715h and continued until the school's opening bell sounded.

This act of recognizing God first transcended to the students within the program. Occasionally, the students had to enter the building before the scheduled time due to inclement weather. The students would show respect to our Bible study and wait patiently outside the door. We could hear students in the hallway speaking to their fellow classmates, stating, "Quiet, be quiet! The sergeants are praying." As Christian believers, we influenced the students' behavior. It is acceptable and necessary to show your faith.

In the year 2003, I sensed restlessness in my spirit. I felt a burning urge to move on and away for C. E. Byrd High School. There was a still, soft voice telling me it was time to move on. I felt a calling to step down from this prestigious high school and transfer to a low-performance high school.

At the low-performing inner-city high school, there is a great need for hardworking and dedicated teachers that are up to the challenge. Teachers of this caliber can bring hope, love, and encouragement into the classroom and pass this on to the students. Parents play a vital part in a student's performance; however, teachers have the ability to jump-start and motivate students. A teacher who sincerely cares about students will earn the child's respect which will, in turn, allow learning to take place.

Many of my associates questioned my motives in wanting to leave C. E. Byrd. There were individuals who investigated whether I was leaving due to a poor performance record. They were proven wrong. Several coworkers said I was crazy to think that I could make a difference in a low-performing school. My calling was clear to me, and this was much bigger than the male ego.

I saw the result of the labors of the low-performing schools. I saw the downcast and frustrated looks of the students who never won a single competition at the different meets they joined. The fact remains that we sometimes have the tendency to see the poor black inner-city kids in a different light as far as the learning process is concerned. *Slow* is usually the word attached to these kids. I wanted to prove the doubters wrong.

There was no turning back for me. Many of my students at C. E. Byrd cried and threatened to transfer out when the news spread that I was leaving. I was going to the low-performing Fair Park High School. That was the place for me. My motto is and remains to be, "If God is your guide—He will provide. And if He leads, He will provide every need."

My first week at FPHS caused resentment to authority and power to surface. I would overhear statements such as "He thinks he is better than us" because I was coming from C. E. Byrd country. That would be just one of the many issues I would have to deal with at the school, but

I knew what the end result would be. Quitting, for me, was never an option.

It was time to address my new cadets after two days of careful observation and evaluation of their strengths and weaknesses. My first speech was somewhat aggressive, but I had to establish my authority and power base. I made it abundantly clear that I had not come to Fair Park to make any new friends. The fact of the matter is—I have too many friends. I had not come to Fair Park for the principal's approval or the SAI's approval or any of the other JROTC instructors. I was there for the students only. Feelings would get hurt, but we would be doing things strictly by the book. I knew how to train winners. I did sense that a few students wanted to challenge my authority, and it would take my making an example of those students on the spot to train them.

I put together a training program with the color guard, drill teams, and the orienteering team. We got busy! It was like being a drill sergeant once again.

Some of the cadets did report my aggressive training style up the chain of command. To no avail did it change my way of doing things. It was still my way or the highway. By this time, some of my cadets were catching on to the way things were going to be done. They came to realize what I had been preaching and what I believed was a possibility. It took a great deal of energy to get the cadets to realize that you get what you train for, and so far, the cadets had been trained only for last place.

After training extensively for two months, it was time to go do battle at the Fall Caddo Parish Blowout Competition. We met early on this particular Saturday morning at the rear end of Fair Park's JROTC training area. The bus driver parked within the gated area. I put on the drill sergeant demeanor and obtained accountability from each student. I proceeded to file the cadets aboard the bus. I had the cadets join hands, and I led them in prayer. This had never been done before. The bus ride took fifteen minutes to reach our destination.

The pressure was at an all-time high. It overwhelmed all the leaders of the different teams. Some of them forgot their names during the competition. My color guard commander became sick to the stomach and could not perform. I could feel my temper beginning to boil. I spoke to this young man in a very stern voice. I knew his needs—they were faith and confidence in him and in God. I also learned the meaning of a low self-image. This young man needed encouragement and determination to finish something started.

Fair Park would win seven trophies that day. I witnessed some of my cadets crying tears of joy as they marched forward to receive their winning trophies. The color guard commander of whom I felt the urge of choking earlier became extremely emotional. The director announced his team had won first place in the Parish, and he was ecstatic. This young man nearly had me crying with him.

Yes, that was the year that C. E. Byrd would have to sit back and take second place in the color guard arena. We beat the team whom I had coached only a few months earlier. The SAI from Byrd did congratulate me, but I thanked God Almighty. On that same day, Fair Park's drill team won the second-place overall trophy for a routine I had put together for them at the very last few days.

The lightbulb of possibility and achievement was now turned on. Inside the cadets' mind, they had come to realize that they were winners and I now had their undivided attention and respect. I could sense that my cadets understood the value of teamwork. I became very proud of them all from that moment on.

Cadet Lee went on to win best individual drill cadet. He was the last cadet standing at the end of the competition. The crowd from Fair Park High School went wild! The principal called me at home that night for the first time to say thanks.

The very next week, I was named Teacher of the Month. I had free meals for a week. I received gifts from other staff members, and my name was placed on the large billboard in front of the school with this acknowledgement of Teacher of the Month.

Byrd's cadets, on the other hand, were trying to devise a plan to retaliate for their loss. This only reinforced the fact for me that God had a purpose for placing me at Fair Park High School. You may ask the question how I knew this to be true. God has many ways of letting us know His plans for our life—we only need to take the time and listen.

I had reaffirmation that that was a divine intervention. The principal at FPHS informed me that he knew my mom from Mississippi Valley State University. She had been the head cook in the university's cafeteria.

My second sign that this was a divine intervention came when I attempted to contact my mom and ask if she could recall Mr. Cooper, my principal. My mom did not answer the telephone. I had dialed Fair Park's phone number. I had never dialed this number before. I explained to the secretary who answered my call that I had dialed the wrong number. These were not coincidences—they were messages for me to heed.

A new year—2004—came. My cadets entered part two of the Parish-level competition. It was again early Saturday morning.

The cadets and I went through our ritual of prayer that had brought us through previously. We set the stage with prayer, accountability, and proceeded by loading the equipment. Prayer was led by Cadet Lee.

The second time out of the shoot, we were better organized than the previous fall competition. The outcome was similar to that particular fall event—we brought home seven trophies. Now, my chain of command and SAI wanted to assign me as the head coach of the rifle team.

10

ONE MARRIAGE, ONE CHILD FOR LIFE

After boot camp, I was authorized a three-day pass, so I ended up going to Texas for the very first time. I really didn't make any solid travel plans, and little did I know that I would end up in a place called Beaumont, Texas.

Robert, a guy whom I had met one morning while on police call (trash detail), had asked me to accompany him to his hometown during this three-day period to which I agreed but had no true intention of actually following through. I think Robert and I had a special bond in that I knew about his personal problem. Robert was a bed wetter, and I would help him switch mattresses after all the other trainees had exited the barracks. We were able to hide this problem from the drill sergeant.

Friday came, and it was payday for all the trainees. We both received our cash and had a few beers while waiting for a cab to take us back to the barracks. We returned to the barracks and packed a small overnight bag, and away we went to the bus station.

We were dressed in our military khaki uniform, and the party was about to get started. We were now in Beaumont, at his father's home. We had plenty of beer, wine, cigarettes, but nowhere to go or no means to get there. Then, Robert called his Aunt "Jerk," who would later become my mother-in-law.

Yes, Aunt Jerk had made gumbo, and we were all invited to partake. We straightened our uniforms and put on our dark mack daddy shades and waited for our means of transport to arrive. There was a total of four army males—Robert, Forrester, Little Murciel, and myself. Forrester and Murciel were two white boys hanging out with two black boys.

Suddenly, I noticed a green Oldsmobile Delta 88 pulling up into the driveway. A young, light skinned black woman was driving with this young, very, very dark-skinned man sitting up front and close to her. The guys and I proceeded to extinguish our cigarettes and headed toward the car.

It was a really short car ride to Robert's aunt's house. The young woman was named Patricia and was the daughter of Robert's aunt. The young man sitting next to her in the vehicle was her boyfriend, and he was on leave from the Marine Corps boot camp. I later learned that he was to become engaged to Patricia.

We arrived at 4410 Raven Street—our destination—and pulled into the driveway. As I entered the home of the people who would later become my in-laws, I found a seat and sat very quietly on the living room sofa. The aroma of gumbo was permeating throughout the house. I scrutinized the young man from the Marine Corps. He eventually spoke to me.

We had discussed and compared the two of the different branches of the Armed Forces—United States Army and the Marine Corps—until Patricia's brother John Jr. entered the room. He was younger than the two of us and a real joker, full of fun and laughter.

John Jr. and the rest of the guys went outdoors after joking around for a few minutes and smoked a few cigarettes. I remained sitting alone in the living room, and this good-looking young, light-skinned, woman approached me. She leaned over me and gently asked if I would do her a favor.

Without asking what it was she wanted me to do, I responded with a complete yes. She handed to me this large trash bag that needed to be carried out to the garbage receptacle located near the garage. Being naïve, I therefore did not give much thought to the actual connection made at that moment—she wanted my undivided attention and she had it.

Everyone at Robert's aunt's house devoured a big bowl of the delicious gumbo. After our appetite was more than satisfied, the guys and I went joyriding. We went to Joseph the Marine corpsman's home, and he introduced us to potent grass (marijuana).

All that partying and getting high caused me to get sick and nauseous. We rode around town, looking for a hotel for the night. Joseph had to pull over and park on the side of the road several times because at least two of us at a time had to throw up. We finally found a hotel, and the manager recognized we needed to check in and get some rest.

We were lying on the floor in the lobby at times. We checked into our room quick, fast, and in a hurry. Later in the evening, we all returned to Robert's aunt Gert's house. By this time, I was too embarrassed to get out of the car and go inside.

The guys went in the house and left me inside the car. Looking outside the car window, I could see a water faucet and connecting hose to the right of the front door. I felt, if I could only get some cool water on my head, I would feel so much better and the car would stop spinning.

I stumbled over to the water hose and sat on the grass next to the window. I proceeded to soak my head with water. The next thing I noticed was, four adult females placing cold towels on my head and speaking words of great pity for me. They asked me how I got into that situation, and they all referred to me as "baby."

That was not a good night for me. I felt so bad because I knew that my mom did not raise me up to be that way. All I wanted to do was get to a bed and never show my face around those parts ever again.

After a good night's sleep, the guys and I swam in the hotel's swimming pool. I found out from John Jr. that his sister Patricia wanted to talk to me. My very first thought and response was, "About what? Did I do something disrespectful while in the home? What in the world would she have to say to me?"

John Jr. just laughed and said, "Don't be crazy, man. She likes you."

My sense of self would not allow me to comprehend that a good-looking girl like Patricia would seriously be interested in an uncool country boy like me. I was interested, however; and I did manage to muster up enough courage to visit the store for which Patricia worked as a cashier later that day. I just could not muster up enough nerve to go through her checkout line, and fear got the best of me. She might have asked me something which would require me to respond.

The truth is that I had programmed myself to believe that I would marry a country girl, and Patricia was not country—she was definitely city. By then, I was certain she felt that I was either uninterested in her or I was too shy.

To my amazement, she gave me a picture of herself, and finally it was really on. But crazy me, instead of keeping the picture for my own pleasure, I mailed it to my mother for her seal of approval. I actually wanted my mom to show her off to my family back home. Patricia would later become the woman whom I would marry and who would mother my only child. My family background consisted a large family with numerous siblings and many different fathers.

This subject goes deep in my makeup and sense of family. I can recall my childhood days while growing up in Mississippi and the dilemma of having to prove my family genes. There was little family resemblance with my siblings, and we had different last names.

In my household, there was a total of four completely different last names; and no father ever stepped up to the plate and staked a claim. There are the Mosleys—myself and a twin sister who died at childbirth—Jaspers, McCurrys, and Browns. I don't feel that last names carry much weight as it relates to who actually fathered us. It really did not matter to us because we knew we were blood sisters and brothers from my mother's womb.

I can't ever remember seeing my father during my lifetime. I never asked my mother if she was married to him or if he ever lived with us. I have only learned of sister and brothers from my father's side of the family until thirty years later. I do know that my father died from a massive stroke. I was an infant at the time of his death.

My birth records were mixed up because the midwife delivered the babies on the plantation. I was listed at one time as the twin who died at childbirth. Later in life, I had to have my birth certificate corrected for my military career. I did not realize at the time that my Heavenly Father never allowed these earthly conditions to become an issue in my life.

Since that time, I have located my extended family in the United States and have assured them that I held no resentment toward them for the past events if my life—having grown up without a father or the lack of their acknowledgement. All is forgiven as the Father has forgiven me. I can honestly and earnestly say that I have no regrets or bitterness of the past. I can now see the hand of God, how He protected me from all the pity parties and ill will.

Returning to the one child point, I promised myself that I would do everything in my power to learn from my past. One of my goals was to marry only once in my life and to father all my children with only one woman. I did have some fears concerning fatherhood and parenting. My determination and love balanced my lack of experience in that department.

I know a child needs both a father and a mother, but in some cases, that is not possible. Nonetheless, we as fathers must try harder and not bail out at the first available opportunity or difficulty. I am so very proud of the fact that my only daughter says that I did well in the father category. My wife of thirty-two years says she could not be happier.

I can only credit my success to God's grace. I have seen numerous families fall apart, but God saved me to fulfill His purpose. The only reason I am opening up to you is because God's grace often goes unnoticed. You may want to stop and look around and find out who is praying for you because I know that I do not and did not deserve the kind of love He gave to me.

It has been over thirty years since I first put the uniform on, and to this day I still wear it. I will probably wear the uniform until the Lord calls me home, and it will remain in the coffin. When you find your God-given purpose, it never becomes work—just blessed service. It brings pleasure to Him, and pleasing Him is all that really matters in this life.

My daughter is a young married woman now. My wife and I really enjoy watching her shape her life and handling the different situations that come her way. The child truly does emulate the parents when entering into adulthood. I just love her and can feel all her growing pains. I would gladly die for my child—similar to what God has done for us.

Now that my child has moved on with her life, my wife and I really enjoy the freedom of just being the two of us in the home. My wife returned to school to become a nurse.

11

THE KEY QUESTION THAT CHANGED MY LIFE

There was something different about Mark. He was never very loud or aggressive and never would complain or use profanity. He was well respected by teachers and students alike. He did not have very much conversation with any particular person, but you somehow knew he was a thinking man. I would later find out that he was a Christian who walked upright in the Lord. Anytime we had concerns or questions of a biblical nature, he would give very detailed answers. I could see that he was really well versed in the Bible and very knowledgeable on history and computers.

After working together for about two and a half years, he had earned my respect for the standard he set as a peacemaker. This impressed me.

He shocked me one day when he spoke up on my behalf. There was a question of whether or not I had properly scheduled bus transportation for a field trip that was to take place. I will never forget that day. This white man had true concern for me.

During this period, my wife and I were at a standstill in our Christian walk. We would sort of hit and miss attending church service at the military-based chapel. We were of the Catholic religion but were not truly committed.

The JROTC staff and I were sitting around at the lunch table when Mark asked a question of Raymond. This man had been a mentor to me from the day I became a member of the JROTC faculty. The question was, *What do you understand it takes for a person to go to heaven?*

At this time, I was going through, in my mind, all the possible answers Raymond might respond; but I knew Mark would give only the biblical answer. Raymond did give many answers, but none of them were acceptable to Mark. I recall at that point in time thanking God that he had not asked me.

Mark asked where attended church. I quickly respond with "On the base" because my wife and I liked the military environment. Mark invited my wife and me to visit his place of worship. He attended Summer Grove Baptist Church.

Out of respect for this person, I said, "Yes, possibly Sunday." He went over the times of the services, located the church route from a city map, and told me they would be looking for me on Sunday. My word has always been my bond.

After explaining that I had given my word to my coworker, Patricia did not seem to like the idea. She just wanted to fulfill a promise I had made. We had visited that Sunday. Mark and Edna Faye, his wife, were both waiting at the entry for us.

We went inside this really huge church; we were amazed by its size. It was by far the largest church I had ever visited, and I later learned that this was true for Patricia. The church choir appeared to have at least two hundred robbed singers. I counted four black faces in the entire congregation. What really captured my attention was the sea of white faces.

Everyone was busy greeting each other, which made us uncomfortable. Our feeling at this point was to get the service over and head home. We did, however, make four more consecutive visits. I found myself being drawn to Summer Grove, even though my wife had not said very much about her feeling for the church or its people. We both had been looking for something wrong with these people.

Each time we visited, we both felt more and more welcome. I would become convinced that the Lord was drawing me into a closer relationship with Him through this body of believers. I also came to realize that this was not my relationship with my wife but between me and God. I prayed that God would start to work on my wife and convince her, if this was a part of His plan. I actually gave her up to Him. It would be our fourth or fifth visit to Summer Grove Baptist Church that I would make a decision that would change our lives forever.

That Sunday morning, crossing Jimmie Davis Bridge from Bossier City into Shreveport, I knew I would not allow another day to go by without my committing my life to God. He was my Lord and Savior. I looked at my wife who was driving the car and told her that I would be going forward that day and committing my life.

After a long moment of silence, she replied, "I wish you would talk to me about these decisions. Please make this a battle, His. In over twenty-two years with my wife, I knew God could do a good work in our marriage.

We both renewed our faith on this Sunday and asked to be baptized as soon as possible. The first Sunday after Christmas, we were baptized, side by side. This would be a life-changing experience for the two of us.

In the first visit to Summer Grove, we did not carry a Bible, and this would not be a problem because those around you would lean over so that you could read one of theirs. In the Catholic Church, the Sunday's lessons were printed on papers located in the pews.

I really liked the pastor at Summer Grove, and I really loved the Sunday Bible study classes. It seemed as if the Word actually took life there, and I understood the teachings. My wife and I really love our church family and our place of worship. We sing in the choir, and I occasionally teach Sunday school class. We enjoy evangelism visits and love our faith. But we both love the Lord more than anything else on this earth.

It is that very question I heard Mark ask Raymond at the lunch table that day that led me to the correct pathway. I am on that pathway now because of God's grace. Understanding Ephesians 2: verse 8 and 9 is vital for anyone desiring to go be with God.

12

COMMITTED TO A
GREATER CALL TO SERVE

We often start projects only to quit or give up after a few failures. My message is simple: be a winner and stop quitting before giving it your very best.

After twenty years of military service, thirty-plus years of marriage, and over fifteen years as an educator, I can say without a doubt that quitting is not an option for me. I am a server, and this is where I find true joy. I felt that it was time to hang up my uniform, and for the first time in my life, I suddenly had to draw unemployment benefits. I felt like a fish out of water for a period of two months while waiting on civilian employment.

The seed for my second career had already been planted years prior to my actual retirement date. Even though I had forgotten about the completed application forms I had forwarded over five years prior, someone remembered and had a purpose for me. The program that I would become employed under would be army JROTC. This program is centered on helping young people become better citizens, and it would require me to continue to model my wonderful military uniform.

A telephone call started the wheels rolling. It was from JROTC region from Tacoma, Washington. It was in a reference to paperwork I had completed over six years prior to my retirement. I was asked to consider completing this process of employment with an interview.

Region had listed four states of which I could visit and have my interview conducted with an interviewing officer. I had not given any thought to a job that requires me wearing another uniform. God had already scheduled transportation and everything else. To my amazement, another retired friend was looking for work and asked if I would ride with him to Shreveport, Louisiana. I suddenly remembered that in Shreveport was one of the interviewing sites; all I had to do was call and let him know that I was coming to his area and needed to complete the record. So that is what I did.

The sergeant major informed me of a list of individuals applying for a job there, but there were no openings. I just wanted to complete the interview, so I forwarded my military files with a sharp photo of myself in uniform. There was a meeting scheduled with director of army instruction Lieutenant Colonel Miller on a Monday morning. Monday finally arrived, and we departed early to ensure that I arrived on time.

I did not realize that I had put on blue socks instead of black, so I had to keep my pants pulled down really low. Upon my arrival at the DAI's office, my friend, who had driven his car, stated that he would wait in the car. The interview lasted three hours, and during the processes of my interview I noticed a really short man in the background. He was trying not to be noticed.

Questions kept coming, and so did the answers. I remembered one question in particular. I had answered it correctly, but the interviewer had to open the book because he was not sure of the answer. We are supposed to learn something new every day; this day, my interviewer learned something new about FM 22-5. It is a field manual governing drill and ceremonies in the military and JROTC.

My intentions were to leave the interview and get back home to DeRidder, Louisiana, before dark. However, I was not looking forward to the long ride home. To my amazement, the DAI asked if I could come back the very next day and visit the eleven high schools in the parish. Initially I thought *no*, but said *yes* instead. It can't hurt to look, can it?

After a good night's rest, I returned. The first school I visited was C. E. Byrd High School. The principal looked me directly in my eyes and said, "I hope you pick me." After a few minutes, I informed Lieutenant Colonel Miller that I did not need to see anymore schools. I was then given the job offer, but the decision of that magnitude needed to be blessed by my wife, so I asked if he would allow me a few days to discuss things with my wife.

It seemed only fair since she had been so faithful in following me around the world for the last twenty years. Perhaps she wanted to focus on her own career. Maybe she did not want to relocate. After all, we had just purchased a house in DeRidder. I then informed him that I would get back with him in three days. My wife, daughter, and I had a long discussion; and the decision was made that Patricia would continue her education in Fort Hood, Texas. My daughter, Demetra, would complete her last year of high school in DeRidder. I would drive to Shreveport to work each day. I would eventually rent an apartment in Bossier City while working at the high school.

Had my wonderful wife not been willing to relocate to Shreveport, Louisiana, I would have easily declined this job offer. God had already blessed me with a wonderful military career, and it was now time for me to focus the unity and stability of my family. No more separations by deployments overseas or field training exercises. My main concern was to give support to the field of work my wife desired for herself; after all, she has supported and put up with me for twenty-plus years of military lifestyle. It takes a really committed spouse to put up with a soldier; and if your marriage is not one of total commitment, military lifestyle will seriously test it.

A thirty-year marriage is very rare these days; and if you have survived your first five years, consider yourself blessed. Many people have written books on the subject of marriage, but none can tell you how to survive this great union. It seems to me that if marriage is so important, why not have special training mandated before a person embarks?

How many people actually understand what it truly means to be in love? Or should a marriage be based on sex alone? The dark side of that is the fact that you will have to come out of the sheets at some point, and you better have something in common with each other than good sex.

Marriages must be grounded on a solid foundation so that when storms of life come, it will not fall apart. You spend thirty years together as best friends, mates, and support systems for one another; and in doing, so you enjoy growing old together.

Just look around at the number of single-parent families in America. Jumping in and out of marriages is a common practice. I consider myself to be a very lucky man to have chosen a woman of whom many men could only dream of having. My wife supported and stood beside me throughout twenty years of military service and is still my number one fan and supporter.

When the military called me to a faraway land, I needed a person who would wait for me and remain faithful, a woman who could keep the home of life functioning in my absence. You need a person who can take care of your children. It doesn't hurt to have a wonderful cook as well. I am blessed to have all of the above.

At the end of the story of thirty years' marriage, the children are grown and gone. They still call home for advice. They will always remain your babies. This is a great time to start a second career—or a first in career, in my wife's case. After following me around the world for twenty years, finally, there was time to do what she has longed to do.

This would require returning to school for a number of years. If you are truly in love, you will really enjoy each other's company. Just to sit and watch television, attend church, walk in the park, go fishing, anything—all this is quality time the two of you can spend together. It is so very important to keep the relationship alive.

It is a really good thing to do as many things as time will permit together. Turn off the television sometimes and just talk. Sometimes a woman does not want answers; she just wants you to listen. Men really enjoy solving problems. But sometimes we need to just be there for her and assure her of our support. Teamwork, support, and encouragement

are more important now than ever before. These are the days for which
you have awaited.

13

BROTHER, BROTHER, WHERE ARE YOU?

My mother had seven children—two boys and five girls. The boys were as different as night is to day. Everybody in town knew my brother Man, but Jim never made a name for himself. Man was always full of action, adventure, and on the wild side.

Jim would graduate from high school and spend the next twenty-plus years serving his country in the military. Man, on the other hand, would spend a large portion of his life behind bars. I pray to God that one day he may experience freedom again.

Our lives would take us in two different paths on a journey of no return. Man was always the adventurous one. He could find trouble no matter where he went. I can recall a time when we were young boys living on the plantation. My mom believed in discipline; she did spare the rod. Man and I would compare the long, blue, and bloody cuts made from Mom's whipping cord. Back then, there was no such thing as child abuse, definitely not in the woods where we lived!

I can recall a particular evening my Mom was disciplining Man for melting my sister's eyeglasses on the wood-burning heater. In between the beating, he suddenly announced that he needed to relieve himself. Mom had no problem allowing us to urinate off the front porch. This time, my brother did the bravest thing. He made a run for the fields where he thought he could hide out in the tall cotton patch. I remember his words prior to his jumping off the porch, "Y'all, I'm gone."

Our dog Dale followed joyfully, thinking it was now playtime. With Dale's barking and Mom dispatching all of us, we quickly tracked Man down, and then his beating would continue. Man and I fight sometimes, and my Mom would make us hug afterward. We grew into adolescence, and Man dropped out of school and moved out of the house to be on his own.

After I graduated from high school, our lives would take a major turn in two different directions. I went on to join the military, while Man would continue working with the lumberjacks, cutting trees.

I know that my decision to join the military was one of the best decisions I have ever made. This was the opportunity and break that I needed. Not only did it give me an opportunity to grow, but it gave me extra money to send home so Mom feels a little relief. It felt good to be able to show a little love and to give back for a change.

After completing both phases of my military training (basic and advance individual), the army sent me to my very first unit of assignment in Fort Hood, Texas. I recall getting that first huge paycheck. I received over five hundred dollars that pay period, mainly because of the travel pay added.

After wrapping the fresh, crisp twenty-dollar bill in yellow paper, I then mailed the ward, which equaled to five hundred dollars, addressing it to Mom. This was not a very smart move on my part, but after a few days had passed, I called home to ensure delivery had been made and Mom had indeed received the five hundred dollars. One of my sisters, Emma, answered the phone; and after hearing what I had to say, she then informed me that Man had made the purchase of a new bike, clothing, and had been on a crazy spending spree. Just prior to the money coming up missing, he had walked to the post office, each day expecting a letter from his girlfriend Tiny. This, added to the fact that he had lost his job, was clear to everyone, as well as me, where the money had gone.

After I had served about a year in the military, my brother could see that the military actually was a good deal, so he decided to join.

The two of us were now stationed at Fort Hood, Texas, but then the unthinkable happen. Man was accused and convicted of rape of a white woman in Texas. This is when I lost the only brother I ever knew. My brother Man is still in jail, but this time he is serving time for statutory rape of a minor in the Texas prison system. I love and miss him deeply. What a relationship we could have had.

14

RACISM AT THE WHITE HOUSE

Yes, I served at the White House. Who would have thought that a young man from the plantations of Mississippi would get an opportunity to serve his country all over the world and at our nation's capital. My duties were to supervise joint service ceremonies at the White House, the Tomb of the Unknown Soldier, and the Pentagon and congressional escort duties around the world. I was assigned to The Old Guard in the military district of Washington, DC, from 1981 to 1984.

It was during my third tour overseas in Germany that I had the honor of meeting members of The Old Guard recruiting team. The team was interviewing overseas and looking for clean-cut soldiers who met the high standards of qualifications for membership. It was actually my commander who thought that I might qualify and selected me for an interview. The team completed all interviews and returned to Washington, DC, to sort through the list of applications. I was selected, and after passing a background investigation, I was given White House clearance access.

My being a country boy, I still had a lot to learn about life in the big cities. I quickly found this out when I returned to the United States and purchased a ticket to Fort Myers. The airport issued me my ticket for Fort Myers, Florida, but I was going to Fort Myers, Virginia, where I was assigned to the Third United States Infantry Regiment, The Old Guard. The airport management in Florida did rectify the problem by putting me up overnight at their expense and then rerouted me the very next day. I did manage to get to my new military assignment.

The first thing that I noticed upon my arrival to The Old Guard was the sea of white faces. I learned that this was no place for your average soldier. All the soldiers had the high and tight haircuts, and they stood tall in their dress blues. This was the time for me to prove myself worthy and make the many adjustments required. I had left my family behind in Texas, but I would send for them after I had settled in and found a place for us to live. While assigned to The Old Guard's honor unit, there were many ceremonies that would be performed at the White House. The honor guard was required at the Pentagon and throughout the nation's capital and the Tomb of the Unknown Soldier.

This is when acts of racism first hit me really hard.

I can recall situations of lower-ranking soldiers calling me by first name. In the military, this is disrespect and punishable under the uniform code of military justice (UCMJ). There were the late-night phone calls— nigger this and nigger that, black this and black that. I would literally pull the plug out of the phone jack. I would have the telephone company change my number to unlisted. The only problem with this situation was that the company's first sergeants alert roster had to be updated anytime a number was changed.

As a result of this continued harassment by members within my ranks, I had to have my phone number changed a total of three times in one month. This only made me more determined to be the best of the best. Even though I knew who the racist soldiers were, I would not give them the pleasure of seeing me break down and sweat.

In the military, you need proof before filing a charge against another soldier. This plot to get rid of me may have come from higher up. I would keep my cool and never allow my performance to slip as a result of what I was experiencing. After many efforts to run me off and out of this mostly white unit, I still found peace. The perpetrators soon realized that I was here to stay. This was the year 1982.

At this time, my platoon sergeant asked me to attend the air assault school located in Fort Campbell, Kentucky. This would be a three-week training course, and I would finish number one and distinguished honor graduate of my class. I would really be noticed by several people now. My assignments would take a major turn for the better from this point forward—NCOIC of the joint services at the White House, congressional escort sergeant, and platoon sergeant of the First Presidential Marching Platoon, to name a few of the many important events and roles throughout my assignment at the nation's capital. Overall, The Old Guard was really a great experience for me, and the skills I learned would remain within me. After three years in Washington, DC, and Fort Myers, Virginia, I would be reassigned by the military and move my family once again.

I wanted to be a drill sergeant. It was 1984, and during the Reagan-Bush inauguration, I would put in my request for drill sergeant school. It was approved. This would come at a time during which my best friend returned to my platoon after he failed the drill sergeants' training school.

I soon came to realize that this would be the hardest school ever for me. I relocated my family to Beaumont, Texas. I had work to do at Fort Benning, Georgia, drill sergeant school. After three months of the hardest training I would ever undergo, I once again excelled. I was awarded the Distinguished Leadership trophy and award.

No one in Washington, DC, Old Guard would have expected this from a country boy. The chain of command notified my command sergeant major in Fort Myers, Virginia, because he would become the speaker at my graduation ceremony. This was not the custom. In the addition, my family would drive down for the event. I had to memorize the drill sergeant's creed. This was not the problem. By then, I could memorize anything. My wife, daughter, mother, in-laws, and niece attended the graduation exercise. This was a day of pride for me. I later found out that every member in my class had voted for me to become the honor graduate of the class of '84.

I did serve two years as a drill sergeant in Fort Benning, Georgia. I also attended airborne training and was later deployed again to Germany. I continued my service to my country and obtained the rank of master sergeant. I attended the United States Sergeants Major Academy and finished my twenty years of service. I decided it was time to retire. Little did I know that my uniform wearing days were not over; it had just begun.

I applied for many jobs at several places. At a prison for a security position, Walmart, the postal office, and law enforcement job training program. I did not hear from any of these. I did receive phone calls from Tacoma, Washington, in reference to a JROTC interview. I had no interest or knowledge on the subject.

This, however, would turn out to be God's purpose and selection of employment for me. You just know when you are where He has placed you. Teaching and training cadets is very similar to being in the army; I got to teach skills that are necessary for life.

15

YOU WERE NO ACCIDENT

After approaching the two-year dating mark, Patricia and I knew that it was time to make a more solid commitment in our relationship. After moments of heated passion, it was becoming very difficult to remain faithful in keeping the promise. The ring had to be place on the finger before sex. I don't think this would have worked had there not been the godly counseling received from our Catholic priest, Father Young.

The understanding was made crystal clear in the early stages of our relationship; however, knowing that Patricia's dad kept his shotgun behind his bedroom door helped keep things in its proper perspective. My religious affiliation was Baptist and Patricia's was Catholic. The two of us completed the two weeks of Catholicism premarital teaching, and

I changed my affiliation to the Catholic faith also. Father Young was always available with sound advice and support.

It was now 1976 in the heated month of May. We were to become married in a few weeks. The weekend bus trips to and from Beaumont to Killeen, Texas, was taking its toll on me. Determined that the next trip to see my future wife would not be taken on a Greyhound bus, I decided to purchase a 1963 Mercury Marquis.

I made a four-hundred-dollar down payment and drove it off the car lot. I was ready and excited about signing out on military leave. I now had my own car and my dream girl and two entire weeks' free time. The only thing that stood in my way of getting married was the long drive to Beaumont, Texas.

The used car salesman actually sold me the car. This was my very first automobile, and he did not inquire as to whether I was a licensed driver. I was not. Full of the excitement of everything that was going on and now owning my first automobile, I put the drive shift in D, and away I went.

The car lot was located in a small country town outside of the city limits. I had plenty of gravel roads to practice on keeping the car in the correct gravel path. I learned to drive before the main freeway leading into the city, and I drove to the apartment I had rented. I had no previous driving experience but was beginning to feel really good about getting the car to the apartment in one piece until I got word from Patricia that her mom sent two boys to help with the drive to Beaumont. This would only be a five-hour trip, but nevertheless John Jr. and Timothy arrived at the bus station on schedule looking excited and ready for a party. Both boys were a bit on the wild side, but I had to maintain a clear head for the upcoming events. John Jr. and Timothy had a few drinks and a little smoke. I actually drove the entire route to Beaumont.

We pulled into the driveway of 4410 Raven Street late in the evening. Patricia and a few of her girlfriends were ready and waiting to take the car for a test drive. Patricia tried to hide the disappointment of the cheap car, but she had to have smelled the scent of what John Jr. and Timothy had been smoking during our longer-than-expected trip.

On June 5, 1976, Patricia and I were married by Father Young. After two days, we were on the road together and headed to our very own place. The car did manage the return trip, but I moved down a few roadside markers on an exit ramp. I did not see any sirens go off or any police cars chasing me, so I asked Patricia to drive the remaining distance.

After our arrival, we found the apartment in a bit of a mess. My army buddy whom I allowed to stay in my apartment for a few days had not controlled his pets very well. I had to go in and clean the apartment while Patricia sat in the car and cried. She cried persistently for three days!

About three months into our marriage, my military unit received notification for a deployment overseas to Germany. This would be a temporary duty assignment (TDY). Spouses and dependent children could not accompany. This was a six-month window. Patricia and I were now faced with the fact that we would be separated for six months.

Many thoughts went through both our minds, and having a child became ever so important. The possibility did exist that I could be called into conflict or be killed in action defending this country. This was a great concern to my wife. It was at this time that we decided to discontinue birth control and make plans to conceive a child.

God did bless us right away, and Patricia was with child. I was able to remain Stateside for most of the pregnancy. Three months prior our first child's, I was deployed to Germany. Some may disagree with military policy, but I am a soldier. And when duty calls, I go. Without a letter from a doctor stating that there were pregnancy complications, staying Stateside would not happen.

Three months into my tour of duty overseas, I received the Red Cross message, "Congratulations, it's a girl, 7 lbs, 3 oz, and 23 inches long, born on 07 June 1977."

My excitement was at an all-time high, and that was by far one of the happiest days of my life. My platoon sergeant allowed me to remain back from field training for a few days to celebrate becoming a father.

Alcohol was very much a part of my celebration during those few days. I must have experienced a blackout or something similar because I can only remember drinking and waking up.

Patricia and I continued to exchange letters and pictures of the baby for the remaining three months throughout this time until I finally returned home. Seeing and holding my own child for the very first time is a moment I will never forget. This feeling is a must for every new father. I experienced many emotions that day, but the one that stands out in my mind is the fear of dropping her or hurting her neck.

She did raise her head for me. My daughter had more hair than I had anticipated, and I just wanted to continue holding her all day and all night. I would secretly awaken her just to play with my baby. How could a father abandon something—someone—so special? Children are truly a gift from God Almighty.

After learning a great deal about parenting, I feel somewhat qualified to say that the key to being successful in this venture is to have the desire to do right by your family. I personally salute all the single mothers because my mom was and she survived, and so can you. My next lesson in Child Rearing 101 is that small children don't understand the meaning of the word *tired*. They want you to also be the pink bunny and keep going and going.

I learned a valuable lesson while pushing my daughter down the street in her new three-wheeler. After pushing this ungrateful child for hours, my back started to hurt, so I decided to take a small break. This was not a good idea; the child actually started crying so passionately that the neighbors were coming out of their house to see what the problem was.

Another thing about babies is that they have a built-in alarm system. My daughter would stare at the doorknob when it was time for me to come home at the end of the work day. And if for some reason I was late, she would howl and act out. Each morning before I would go to work for physical training, I would check her in her room across the hall. Most of the time, she would be waiting with those glowing eyeballs in the dark, staring at me from the crib, and I loved every minute of it.

The last event that I will mention is the time I challenged my wife's job as babysitter. Well, it looked easy enough, so I would babysit while my wife would visit the Laundromat. I completely bathed my child, toweled her dry, powdered her down, and headed to the refrigerator for a cold beer as a reward for my good work.

The mission didn't go as planned because when my back was turned, my child crawled back into the dirty water and I had to start over again. Mopping all the water out the carpet was a major task. Let them know that they were no accident!

CPSIA information can be obtained
at www.ICGtesting.com
Printed in the USA
FFOW02n0832250318
45910586-46807FF